Our Father in Heaven

Our Father in Heaven

MARILYN B. HARBIN

Marilyn B. Harbin

Providence House Publishers
PROVIDENCE PUBLISHING CORPORATION
FRANKLIN, TENNESSEE

Printed in the United States of America

10   09   08   07   06   1   2   3   4   5

ISBN-13: 978-1-57736-377-4
ISBN-10: 1-57736-377-9

Cover and page design by Joey McNair

PROVIDENCE HOUSE PUBLISHERS
an imprint of
Providence Publishing Corporation
238 Seaboard Lane • Franklin, Tennessee 37067
www.providence-publishing.com
800-321-5692

To the memory of my husband,
the late Dr. J. William Harbin,
and to my sons Bill and Ben,
for the love, prayers, inspiration, and
encouragement they have given to me throughout my life

"The whole light of life is captured in this rainbow of seven petitions found in the Lord's Prayer."

—Helmut Thielicke

—ᐤ Contents ᐤ—

—⌒ *Preface* ⌒—

Prayer has always been a vital part of my life. I remember, as a very young child, my mother always had prayer with me before going to bed. These early memories and the value of prayer linger with me and have become even more important to me in my Christian walk throughout these seventy-nine years of my life.

There are many prayers recorded in the Bible, but the most meaningful prayer to me is the one I memorized as a child. It is the model prayer Jesus taught his disciples to pray, the Lord's Prayer, found in Matthew 6:9–13 and in Luke 11:2–4.

While reading the Lord's Prayer in a church bulletin, I realized that I wanted and needed to gain a better understanding into the meaning of this beautiful prayer.

I hope that the explanations, thoughts, and related Scripture passages contained herein will spark within each of us a renewed appreciation for this significant prayer and enrich our prayer lives.

—⌒ ⌒—

One day when Jesus was praying, one of his disciples said to him, "Lord, teach us to pray" (Luke 11:1 NIV). As Jesus answered, he unfolded a rainbow of seven petitions giving a model prayer known as the Lord's Prayer. It encompasses all of life—great things, small things, spiritual things, material things, inward things, and outward things. It is not limited nor is it exclusive to any one religious group. It can be spoken by everybody, in every situation, in any place in the world. However, it specifically takes on meaning for anyone who is committed to the Savior, Jesus Christ.

The Lord's Prayer is so familiar to many people that there is a constant temptation to pray it mechanically and thoughtlessly. The purpose of this book is to help those of us who repeat the Lord's Prayer often to rediscover the depth of meaning and the beautiful way it addresses all of our spiritual and physical needs.

The first three petitions elevate our thoughts to God and the glory of God. The last four petitions relate to our needs and necessities in the present (food), in the past (forgiveness), and in the future (trials)—namely, resisting temptation and deliverance from evil.

In an amazing way, this prayer teaches us to bring our lives to God, and to bring God into our lives.

—⌁ Acknowledgments ⌁—

I want to express my appreciation to Dr. William J. Purdue, retired minister and educator, for reading the manuscript of *Our Father in Heaven* and making significant and helpful suggestions; to Bill and Julie Harbin, my older son and his wife, who gave me my first computer and taught me computer skills, making it possible for me to type the original text; and to Ben and Janet Harbin, my younger son and his wife, for reading the original manuscript and making invaluable recommendations regarding content.

⌒ The Lord's Prayer ⌒

Our Father, who art in heaven,
Hallowed be thy name.

Thy kingdom come.

Thy will be done on earth,
As it is in heaven.

Give us this day our daily
bread.

And forgive us our trespasses,
As we forgive those who trespass against us.

And lead us not into temptation,
But deliver us from evil.

For thine is the kingdom, and
the power, and the glory, forever.

Amen.

—Matthew 6:9–13

OUR FATHER, WHO ART IN HEAVEN, HALLOWED BE THY NAME

Since it is Jesus who teaches us to pray this prayer, it is important to understand that everything Jesus says is a reflection of the heart of God. It is also important, as we approach God, to examine our lives and come with a sincere heart.

First, we need to be fully aware that we are addressing our Father. The remarkable part is that through the acceptance of Jesus into our lives, we become sons and daughters of God and sisters and brothers in Christ. This gives us a close relationship to him. Therefore, we can truly address God as OUR FATHER.

God's dwelling place is in heaven, and as we pray, OUR FATHER, WHO ART IN HEAVEN, we come into the presence of a God who loves us as his children, and he is a holy God and a God of

1

power. Therefore, we place side by side the love of God and the power of God.

God's nature and character deserve a unique place in our lives. God deserves our highest praise and Jesus teaches us in this first petition to pray: HALLOWED BE THY NAME.

We respect God. We bow in awe and reverence before God. The key word here is reverence. In reverencing God, it is important to understand and believe in four essential truths:

1. God exists as a source of life. Just as the sun is a necessary source for our physical lives, God is the necessary source for our spiritual lives.

2. God provided a way for each of us to become his child by sending his son, Jesus, to die for us. Through belief in Jesus we can break out of darkness and come into the sunlight of God's forgiveness and love. We can feel the warmth of his presence. "Hallow" means to look upon as holy. God is holy and just.

3. God values our fellowship with him. We need a constant awareness of God. We need to give God the reverence that his nature and character deserve.

4. God desires our obedience and submission to his ways. We honor God and let him work in our lives.

This is what we pray for when we pray: HALLOWED BE THY NAME.

We need a constant awareness of the brightness and warmth of God's presence.

Petition II

THY KINGDOM COME

The kingdom of God is his spiritual reign over the universe. It begins in the heart of the believer and is a very personal matter. Jesus said in Luke 17:21, "the kingdom of God is within you" (NIV). It can also be said that the kingdom of God is where Jesus Christ is.

When Jesus teaches us to pray for the coming of the kingdom, it is a twofold petition. First, Jesus is concerned about everyone. There are people everywhere who need comfort when in sorrow, help and healing in times of suffering and sickness, compassion and encouragement when broken-hearted or troubled, and kindness and helpfulness during times of need.

It is important for us to be aware of the opportunities we have to bring comfort, help, compassion, and kindness to people in the name of Jesus. We can partner with God in advancing his purpose and in the growth of his kingdom by showing our concern for others and by using our gifts and abilities in our own unique ways to proclaim the kingdom of God.

Second, when Jesus was on this earth, he knew he needed help to fulfill his mission. He chose twelve disciples, and in Luke 9:2, the Bible tells us that "he sent them out to proclaim the kingdom of God" (TEB).

The growth of the kingdom of God is gradual and progressive. It is like a seed planted in the ground that must be nurtured and cared for as it grows, becomes a live plant, and bears fruit.

All people who believe in Jesus are to bear spiritual fruit. We find in Galatians 5:22 that the fruits of the Spirit are "love, joy, peace, patience, kindness, goodness, faithfulness, gentleness, and self-control" (NIV).

To pray THY KINGDOM COME challenges us to bear spiritual fruit in our daily lives and to plant the seed of the Good News that God offers new life and growth to everyone who accepts the invitation to come to Jesus, receive him into their lives, and become a part of the kingdom of God.

We need to show concern for others, bear spiritual fruit, and share the Good News of Jesus.

THY WILL BE DONE ON EARTH, AS IT IS IN HEAVEN

This single petition embraces three significant concepts for us to think about as we pray. First, God's plan was for all people to live in a close relationship with him and to seek his will and guidance daily. Also, God has a plan for each individual person. It starts with a relationship with Jesus Christ and our willingness to focus on using our unique abilities for God. Jesus teaches us to pray THY WILL BE DONE for all people and for each individual person.

Second, we live on Earth. Those who have gone on to be with the Lord have reached perfection, but those of us who are still on Earth are taught by Jesus to pray: THY WILL BE DONE ON EARTH.

Life on Earth is temporary. Seeking to do God's will on Earth gives life meaning, purpose, and motivation. It also prepares us for eternity.

Knowing that life on Earth is temporary presents to each of us an urgency and a challenge to pay attention to what is going on inside us as well as what is going on around us. Our lives need to demonstrate inner courage and commitment even in the midst of the numerous and various hardships or difficult situations that may be around us.

It is important to know that God loves us, cares about us, and is watching over us all the time. He sees our responses to our problems as well as our successes. Many times going through difficult times prepares us for future responsibilities and opportunities as servants of God.

Third, the phrase AS IT IS IN HEAVEN reaffirms and makes clear that the perfect will of God is being done in heaven. We are taught to pray that we may carry out God's plan as faithfully here on Earth as the angels and saints do in heaven so that God's purpose will be accomplished in this world as well as the next.

In Psalm 33:11 we read, "But his [God's] plans endure forever; his purposes last eternally" (TEV). As we determine to follow God's will here on Earth, we need to keep a vision of eternity and value it in our lives as we pray: THY WILL BE DONE ON EARTH, AS IT IS IN HEAVEN.

We need to have inner courage and commitment in our hearts to follow God's way and keep a vision of eternity.

GIVE US THIS DAY OUR DAILY BREAD

L ike the arch of a beautiful rainbow, this model prayer goes all the way from prayer for the coming of the kingdom and preparing for eternity to prayer for our daily bread. The greatest things and the smallest things are included in the Lord's Prayer.

In the progression of this prayer, note that we are to honor God before we pray for ourselves. This fourth petition, GIVE US THIS DAY OUR DAILY BREAD, is the first petition that comes after elevating our thoughts in worship and commitment to our Father. It reveals how realistic, compassionate, and understanding God is about our needs and necessities in our everyday lives on Earth.

When we take note that this part of the prayer is a simple petition for our everyday needs, certain tremendous truths emerge.

First, even though God's majesty and greatness are huge, God is still concerned about even the smallest things in our daily lives.

Second, God encourages us to bring all of our needs, concerns, fears, desires, joys, and heartaches to him.

Third, living one day at a time strengthens us to have faith and trust in God for future needs.

Fourth, in providing our daily bread, God needs our efforts and cooperation. Our diligent work and God's bountiful provisions must be combined.

Fifth, as God provides for us daily we are to share with others.

Sixth, our Father is always available to us and delights in supplying our needs and necessities.

Just as we need physical daily bread, we also need spiritual daily bread. This spiritual food comes from the Word of God. We need to feast daily on his Word to be healthy children of God.

Reading God's Word with understanding provides encouragement, comfort, and guidance, as well as the opportunity to meditate and pray.

In Psalm 62:8, God extends an invitation to "Pour out your hearts to Him" (NIV), and in Psalm 66:19, he gives us assurance that "God has surely listened and heard my voice in prayer" (NIV).

We need to bring all our needs to God—great, small, physical, and spiritual.

AND FORGIVE US OUR TRESPASSES, AS WE FORGIVE THOSE WHO TRESPASS AGAINST US

Jesus taught us to pray for our physical and spiritual necessities and then extended the prayer to include a need affecting the mind and heart of each individual. It is the need for forgiveness.

God's forgiveness is a gracious gift. In order to receive it, each person must have genuine sorrow for wrong deeds and must show forgiveness toward others. Jesus wants us to find peace in our minds and hearts. This peace comes through God's forgiveness to us and our forgiveness to others.

All creation was corrupted when Adam and Eve made a choice in their minds and hearts to disobey God. Therefore, God made provision for us to have forgiveness and peace. In Colossians 1:19–20 (TEV) we read:

For it was by God's own decision that the Son [Jesus] has in himself the full nature of God. Through the Son, then, God decided to bring the whole universe back to himself. God made peace through his Son's death on the cross and so brought back to himself all things, both on earth and in heaven.

The cross on which Jesus was crucified falls like a bridge across the deep gap between unforgiveness and forgiveness. When we invite Jesus into our minds and hearts, he takes us by the hand and walks with us across that bridge from the darkness of unforgiveness into the light of the forgiveness of God.

This approach to the fifth petition becomes more personal as we pray: AND FORGIVE US OUR TRESPASSES, AS WE FORGIVE THOSE WHO TRESPASS AGAINST US.

It is easy to ask God for forgiveness for ourselves, but often difficult to forgive others. However, Jesus teaches us in this petition that to receive forgiveness we must first forgive others; human forgiveness and divine forgiveness are interconnected.

Showing genuine forgiveness to others is much easier if one tries to understand the other person. In human forgiveness, extending an outstretched arm and a warm handshake in love can be a bridge of forgiveness from hurt to healing, bringing freedom and peace.

Jesus taught this prayer to his disciples. Even though they were followers of Jesus, they were still human—they were imperfect and needed divine forgiveness and cleansing from daily sins.

As humans, we make blunders in our choices, attitudes, and relationships. We, too, need divine forgiveness by asking God to forgive us and cleanse us from our daily sins. As children of God, we can be sure that he will forgive us when we sincerely pray: AND FORGIVE US OUR TRESPASSES, AS WE FORGIVE THOSE WHO TRESPASS AGAINST US.

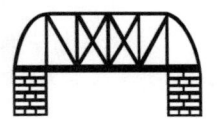

We need to bridge any gap of disobedience or hurt by receiving forgiveness from God and extending forgiveness to others.

Petition VI

AND LEAD US NOT INTO TEMPTATION,

J esus understands that temptations will come to everyone. Satan is real and is constantly fighting against God's purpose for our lives. Temptation itself is not a sin, but yielding to it is.

In this model prayer, Jesus shows his concern for everyone as he teaches us to pray: AND LEAD US NOT INTO TEMPTATION. This petition opens up several channels of thought for us to consider.

- It is a plea that God will spare us from needless temptation, deceit, or testing which might lure us into doing wrong.

- It is a prayer asking God to help us recognize temptation and give us strength to overcome it.

- It alerts us to the reality that temptation comes into our individual minds through desires, doubts, deception, and disobedience.

- It challenges us to possess the courage to show the right attitude in difficult situations and to have a good attitude toward other people as a defense against temptation.

- It reminds us that in overcoming temptation one needs to have knowledge to know right from wrong, the will or desire to do what is right, and the determination to make good decisions.

A great and precious truth about temptation is that it is not designed to make us fall. It should help us to become stronger and better as we resist temptation.

As we pray this petition, God not only hears us, but God promises to be with us as we go through temptations. He will give us strength and endurance and will provide a way out. This promise is found in 1 Corinthians 10:13 (TEV):

God keeps his promise, and he will not allow you to be tested beyond your power to remain firm; at the time you are put to the test, he will give you the strength to endure it, and so provide you a way out.

We need to stop, think, and recognize the reality of temptation and choose to do right.

Petition VII

BUT DELIVER US FROM EVIL

Behind the temptations that come to us is Satan, the evil one. He is deceitful, a master of disguise, and always works against the plan of God. Jesus knows how dangerous the evil one is, so he teaches us to pray: BUT DELIVER US FROM EVIL.

A positive way to approach this petition is to remember that the evil one is a force or power that can be resisted. We must do our part to resist and not give in to evil. We cannot do it alone; we must rely on God's Word and God's presence.

1. Reading and understanding God's Word will help us resist evil. Jesus was tempted by Satan and resisted each temptation. He responded to each temptation by quoting Scripture. The Word of God is powerful and helps us drive away evil.

2. It is important to stay in close fellowship with God through sincere prayer to receive guidance in resisting encounters with the evil one. Just before the arrest, trial, and crucifixion of Jesus, he looked toward heaven and poured out his heart to God in prayer. This beautiful and meaningful prayer by Jesus for his disciples is found in John 17:15, "My prayer is not that you take them out of the world, but that you protect them from the evil one" (NIV).

What a wonderful example Jesus gave us. May each of us look to heaven and pour out our hearts to God for protection from the evil one.

3. Being obedient to the Word of God can help us resist evil. May we let these verses be a challenge to us to be obedient, to be guided by the Holy Spirit, and to follow God's way.

> "Do not be overcome by evil, but overcome evil with good."
>
> —Romans 12:21 (NIV)

> "Away from me, you evildoers, that I may keep the commands of my God."
>
> —Psalm 119:115 (NIV)

> "By all means use your judgment, and hold on to whatever is really good. Steer clear of evil in any form."
>
> —1 Thessalonians 5:21–22 (PMG)

> "Whoever wants to enjoy life and wishes to see good times, must keep from speaking evil and stop telling lies. He must turn away from evil and do good; he must strive for peace with all his heart."
>
> —1 Peter 3:10–11 (TEV)

> "Submit yourselves, then to God. Resist the devil (the evil one) and he will flee from you."
>
> —James 4:7 (NIV)

Reading and understanding God's Word, seeking the guidance of the Holy Spirit, praying sincerely, and being obedient to God give us positive ways to resist the evil one as we pray: BUT DELIVER US FROM EVIL.

We need to pray, read the Bible, and ask for God's guidance to help us resist temptation.

FOR THINE IS THE KINGDOM, AND THE POWER, AND THE GLORY, FOREVER. AMEN.

The seven petitions in the Lord's Prayer are found in Matthew 6:9–13. The source for the last sentence in this prayer is found in 1 Chronicles 29:11 (NIV).

> Yours, O Lord, is the greatness and the power and the glory and the majesty and the splendor, for everything in heaven and earth is yours. Yours, O Lord, is the kingdom; you are exalted as head over all.

The majesty and meaning of this Old Testament Scripture has been captured in a beautiful way to lift our hearts in praise to God in closing our prayer with a paraphrase of this verse.

It is important to realize that, after praying the Lord's Prayer, we have experienced the unique privilege of speaking with our Father. It may take a lifetime of praying this prayer before it begins to dawn on us the kind of God we have.

We can never learn how mighty and glorious he is unless we learn from experience that he really does meet all of our daily needs. God reaches down to us in the midst of heartaches and frustrations and gives us strength and hope. He really does forgive our trespasses and gives us a new heart to be able to forgive others. As we constantly draw from God's source of power and glory, we learn that it is continuous and everlasting. God's goodness is always available and plentiful.

Just as the conclusion to this prayer breaks forth in praise, our repeated use of the Lord's Prayer leads us to praise God. By doing this, we can find release from momentary concerns and lift our thoughts to the God of heaven and eternity.

The Lord's Prayer begins with praise to our Father and comes around in a full circle to end with praise to God, our Father, as we pray: FOR THINE IS THE KINGDOM, AND THE POWER, AND THE GLORY, FOREVER. AMEN.

We need to give praise to God for his greatness, power, glory, and splendor.

MAKING THE
LORD'S PRAYER YOUR OWN

The Lord's Prayer summarized as Personal
Petitions to God, Our Father

**OUR FATHER, WHO ART IN HEAVEN,
HALLOWED BE THY NAME.**
> Father, I give praise and
> reverence to you,
> and pray that I will always
> have a constant awareness of
> the brightness and warmth of
> your holy presence.

THY KINGDOM COME.
> Father, I want to partner with
> you in the growth of your kingdom
> by showing concern for others,

bearing spiritual fruit, and
sharing the Good News of Jesus.

**THY WILL BE DONE ON EARTH,
AS IT IS IN HEAVEN.**
Father, grant me inner
courage and commitment to
always follow your way.
May I keep a vision of
eternity in my mind and
value it in my life.

GIVE US THIS DAY OUR DAILY BREAD.
Father, I put my trust in
you and bring all of my
needs to you—great, small,
physical, and spiritual.

**AND FORGIVE US OUR TRESPASSES,
AS WE FORGIVE THOSE WHO
TRESPASS AGAINST US.**
Father, help me to bridge
any gap of disobedience or
hurt I have caused to you
or others by receiving your
forgiveness and by
extending forgiveness
to others.

AND LEAD US NOT
INTO TEMPTATION,
>Father, provide me with
>insight to stop, think, and
>recognize the reality of
>temptation and to have the
>determination to
>choose to do right.

BUT DELIVER US FROM EVIL.
>Father, guide me in the
>understanding and use of the
>message of the Bible as the
>Holy Spirit leads. Help
>me to be obedient to
>your Word, and to resist evil.

FOR THINE IS THE KINGDOM, AND THE
POWER, AND THE GLORY, FOREVER. AMEN.
>Father, I give praise to you
>for your greatness, power,
>glory, and splendor.

Values to treasure within each petition of the Lord's Prayer

Petition I—Praise
Petition II—Sharing
Petition III—Commitment
Petition IV—Trust
Petition V—Forgiveness
Petition VI—Determination
Petition VII—Obedience
Closing—Praise

➤ Bibliography ➤

Books

Thielicke, Helmut. *Our Heavenly Father*. New York, N.Y.: Harper & Row, 1960.

Warren, Rick. *The Purpose Driven Life*. Grand Rapids, Mich.: Zondervan, 2002.

Commentaries

Barclay, William. *The Gospel of Luke*. Philadelphia, Penn.: Westminster Press, 1956.

Barclay, William. *The Gospel of Matthew*. Vol. 1. Philadelphia, Penn.: Westminster Press, 1958.

Pfeiffer, Charles, and Everett Harrison. *The Wycliffe Bible Commentary*. Chicago, Ill.: Moody Press, 1962.

Dictionaries

Britannica World Language Dictionary. Vols. 1–2. Chicago, Ill.: Encyclopaedia Britannica, Inc., 1959.

Kauffman, Donald T. *The Dictionary of Religious Terms*. Westwood, N.J.: Fleming H. Revell Company, 1967.

Webster's Dictionary and Thesaurus. Ivyland, Penn.: POP-M Publications, 1989.

Sermons

Harbin, J. William. "The Growth of the Kingdom of God." (Mark 4:26–29). Personal file 60.

———."How to Overcome Temptation" (1 Cor. 10). Personal file 858.

———. "More Luscious Fruit" (Gal. 5: 22–26). Personal file 871.

—ᥣ *About the Author* ᥤ—

Marilyn B. Harbin is the wife of the late Dr. J. William Harbin, who was a minister for more than fifty years. As a pastor's wife, she supported her husband in all phases of ministry and was especially active in the music program of the church.

She earned a bachelor of music degree from the Southern Baptist Theological Seminary School of Music and a bachelor of science degree in education from the University of Tennesseee.

Mrs. Harbin was an elementary school teacher in Maryville, and later, Franklin, Tennessee, for a total of fourteen years.

She currently resides in Franklin, and is the mother of two grown sons.